DAILY DOSE
Devotional

April Williams

To Iris

Unless otherwise indicated, all Scripture
quotations are from the King James
Version of the Bible.

Daily Dose Devotional
Dynamic Direction for a Successful Life
ISBN 978-1-64621-005-3
Copyright © 2019 by April Williams
Beyond Publishing & Promotions USA

wisdomforbeyond.com

Printed in the United States of America

Table of Contents

<u>Dedication</u>

To my mother, Sherron Thomas, who taught me to fight my battles on my knees. I love you.

To my five sons—I love you with all my heart!

To Drs. Paul & Angel Crites. Your love and wisdom mean the world to me!

To my best friend, Joy Catoe. I don't deserve your amazing friendship. Love you more!

To my husband, Todd. Thank you for your love & support. I am so glad we are together on this journey. Love you so much!

Day 1
(Deuteronomy 28:13)
Mindset

Have you ever gotten a song stuck in your head?

It plays in the background of your thoughts all day. Did you know that you have an internal dialogue that plays in the background of your mind?

Think about it for a moment.
You have a system of belief about yourself.

Do you think you are a failure or that you cannot succeed? Your mindset will become a filter from which you interpret life experiences.

Didn't get a job you applied for?
You conclude you are a failure.

A spouse or friend disappoints you?
You immediately feel unloved.

The greatest battle you will ever face is in your mind. Your mind is the womb of your destiny. Identify your internal dialogue and change your mindset to what God says about you.

Remember:

☕ Identify your internal dialogue.

☕ Find out what God says about you.

☕ Train your mind to focus on success and winning.

Day 2
(John 4)
Greatness in others

Do you see the greatness in others?

Greatness is all around you. You must look for it, expect it, and celebrate it. Pursue greatness and reward it whenever you find it.

Everyone wants to feel important. Deep within every human heart is the desire to be celebrated. Is your presence improving others' lives?

Can you see the greatness and potential in even the most unlovable person?
Jesus saw the worth in the most despised and rejected. He stopped and conversed with the Samaritan woman at the well in John chapter 4.

The Samaritans were despised by the Jews, but Jesus took the time to speak just to her. Many in that city believed because of her testimony.

Can you see others how God sees them?

See the greatness that is all around you.

<u>Remember</u>:

☕ Recognize the greatness around you.

☕ Those around you can become great. Be their bridge to greatness.

☕ Recognize and reward the achievements of others.

Day 3
(Ephesians 3:20)
Dream Big

Your dream should be too big to contain.

What is your dream?
What energizes you and makes you feel alive?

Sit down today and create a list of what you dream of doing. Your dream should be big enough to consume you, or it will not motivate you.

Many times, we surround ourselves with tasks that we hate or jobs we dread, never focusing on what we love. Life is too short to work at a job that you loath.

God promises us that He will do far above all that we could ask, hope, or think.

We expect too little.
We think so small.

Delight yourself in the Lord, and He will give you the desires of your heart.

So, what are your desires?
Sit down and write them out today!

Remember:

☕ What energizes you?

☕ What do you dream of doing?

☕ Write it down!

Day 4
(Philippians 4:8)
Focus

Your focus is everything.

Dictionaries define focus as the center of interest or activity. Your focus becomes where your mind rests, the center of life's thoughts.

Where your focus goes, your energy flows.

You must choose if you desire your energy to flow to the problem or the solution.

Have you ever been carsick? I get motion sickness if I am riding in a car, while attempting to focus on an object as the landscape zooms by within my peripheral vision.

Improper focus will make you sick—sick of life. Small tasks become arduous, and dread consumes your day.

When you choose a focus, you choose a master.

Choose to focus on solutions, not on problems. You cannot focus on everything, but focus is everything!

Remember:
Focus decides

 Direction
 Destiny
 Success

Day 5

(James 3:2)

Conversation

A conversation can transform people and relationships. Communication can change situations, especially conflict.

Conflict is all around us.

How are you navigating the tumultuous waters of conflict and offense? We can approach conflict by avoiding it, handling it poorly, or facing the conflict and handling it well.

Often when the stakes are the highest, we crash and burn. As much as others need to change, or we desire them to change, the only person you can change is you.

In a conflict, we need to focus on understanding the other person, not changing him.

In the heat of an argument, we divert to winning the argument, punishing the other person, or avoiding the entire situation in order to keep the peace. Winning an argument may cost you a relationship.

Aiming accusations at another builds massive walls of hurt and bitterness.
When we clam up to just keep the peace, we lose the opportunity to talk and gain an understanding.

<u>Remember:</u>
Communication Killers

 Winning
 Punishing
☕ Keeping the peace

Day 6
(1 Corinthians 14:40)
Disorder

Your greatest challenge in leadership is disorder.

- ☠ Disorder delays and distracts.
- ☠ Disorder is very destructive.
  It saps your energy and creates stress.

What in your life is out of order?
How is your life arranged?
Does your life facilitate productivity?

Don't blame others when your life is in disarray.
- ☑ Take responsibility.
- ☑ Take inventory of everything in your life.

The atmosphere you permit determines the product you produce.

Small steps of order will yield success.
Create habits of order.
Do not permit chaos-it will cost you.

Moving toward order will expose things and people in your life that do not belong.

Order positions you for increase and promotion. You cannot handle increase in the midst of chaos.

Reclaim a life of order.

<u>Remember</u>:
To establish order

- ☕ Recognize chaotic conditions.
- ☕ Respond quickly to chaos.
- ☕ Reclaim a life or order.

Day 7
(Proverbs 24:16)
Failure

You will fail.

Failure is inevitable, but it doesn't have to be fatal. Failure isn't final. Just get up.

The reality is that failure will occur throughout your life more than success.

You must change your perspective in the midst of a seeming defeat. Failure is an opportunity to learn.

In fact, failure can be your greatest teacher. Also, don't rehearse past failures. Don't dwell on them.

Turn off auto-play. Stop talking about what you want others to forget. You cannot walk into your future when you are tethered to the past.

You are so much more than your mistakes!

<u>Remember</u>:
When dealing with failure

☕ Understand we all fail.

☕ Make failure your greatest teacher.

☕ Refocus and move on.

Day 8
(Job 5:17)
Change

Leaders are agents of change.

The word change means to make or become different; transform.

You will never correct what you are unwilling to confront.

Where you compromise, you condone. Correction is the shortest road to success.

Conflicts abound all around us, but when you resolve conflicts quickly, you create a sense of hope around you. Anything permitted increases. So, take inventory of your life. What is breaking your focus? What is draining your energy?

If you are dissatisfied with a situation, change it.
If you cannot change it, change your perspective about it.

At times, people don't change, because they enjoy the drama and the attention their problems provide them.

You can expend energy whining & complaining, or you can expend energy correcting & changing.

Remember:

☕ You can't change what you tolerate.

☕ Strive to change your situation or your perspective.

☕ Correction is the shortest road to success.

Day 9
(Psalm 136)
Goodness of God

You know that God is good, but do you live in His goodness?

The word in Hebrew means loving, merry, pleasant, precious, prosperity, gracious, and sweet.

Do you live in the love, merriment, graciousness, sweetness, and prosperity of God?

We often doubt that God will bless us, because we don't know His goodness. When you live in His goodness, it overflows to others.

The world needs to see the goodness of God; it leads us to repentance.

When you go to the store, work, restaurant, or school, is God's goodness on display?

We love to visit a certain restaurant in our hometown, and a waitress there told us that Christians on Sunday were usually the rudest and cheapest customers.
What kind of witness is that? Are you a good experience?
Is God's goodness on display in your life?

Live in His goodness!

<u>Remember</u>:
Living in His goodness

☕ Brings others to repentance.

☕ Overflows to others.

☕ Creates an abundance in your life.

Day 10
(Proverbs 31:22)
Look the part

Look the part.

Successful people understand the power of presentation. People see you before they hear you.

First impressions matter.
Dress for the job you desire, not the job you currently have. You are a constant message board. Your appearance creates a climate around you.

I educate people on how to approach me by how I dress. At work, I wear a nametag to clearly communicate that I am the manager. I dress nicely to display that I am a person of authority.

The quality of your preparation will determine the quality of your performance. Your attire affects how you feel and perform.

When you have a job interview, dress appropriately; you will feel confident.

I once had an employee candidate show up wearing flip flops. Don't do it. Flip flops are standard issue in South Carolina, but do not wear them to interviews.

Successful individuals understand the power of presentation!

<u>Remember</u>:

- ☕ Look the part.
- ☕ Dress for your future.
- ☕ Consider the message you are sending to others.

Day 11
(Proverbs 10:4)
Poverty

"Poor is a state of mind. Broke is a place you're just passing through."
                                    —Dave Ramsey

The amount of money you make is not the key factor in your current financial state. It is your belief system.

Money follows a belief system. If you continue to approach money in the same manner, you will keep getting the same result. What is your belief system?

Our mindset is often shaped by past experiences or molded by our parents. I hear people say, *"I am never going to get ahead. It's always something- one step forward and two steps back."*

Is that what you believe?
Identifying your belief system and who shaped it is crucial.

Why? Your belief system is either promoting you or demoting you. In fact, what you believe about money governs your behavior and shapes your financial future.

**You cannot prosper and
have a poverty mindset.**

Remember:

☕ Poverty is a state of mind.

☕ Money follows a belief system.

☕ Your belief system governs your financial behavior.

Day 12
(Proverbs 1:5)
Listen

Listening is dynamic.

The word in Hebrew means to listen carefully & intelligently – to pay attention. The word conveys intensity.

What is the single most important action you perform in a conversation?
Listening.

Dean Rusk said, *"One of the best ways to persuade others is with your ears – by listening to them."*

To gather all of the information, you must intelligently pay attention. People rarely express everything. Listen carefully to learn.

Listening allows you to explore others' paths. Invite others to share their minds.

This can be challenging in a conflict. Create a safe atmosphere for individuals to express their stories. Be curious, even if the person is angry. Pause and investigate his story. Avoid overreacting or becoming defensive.

Ask questions. The person who asks the questions controls the conversation.

Don't reciprocate unhealthy communication. Listen and respond.

<u>Remember:</u>
To be a good listener

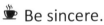 Be sincere.
 Be curious.
 Be patient.

Day 13
(Ephesians 4:26)
H.O.T. Conversations

"Make tense conversations H.O.T.
Honest. Open. Two-way." –Dan Oswald

How can we keep conversations open? Move
from blame to contribution.

☠ Blame is an action that deserves
punishment.

☑ Contribution is an act that may or may
not deserve punishment.

Contribution maintains neutrality and allows
you to objectively examine what you did to
contribute to the situation. What was your
role? Regardless of who seems to be at fault,
each person owns a contribution, even if the
contribution was inaction.

If I approach a conflict with blame, I excuse myself from my actions. That doesn't work. Contribution makes you a team and propels you to find a solution together. Many times, we promote teamwork, until a conflict arises. Then it is gloves off and every man for himself!

Work together for a resolution.
Each person must acknowledge his contribution to the situation, resolve it, and move on. When you become aware of your part, apologize for a specific behavior.

Keep your conversations H.O.T!

<u>Remember</u>:
To maintain openness in communication

 Avoid blame.
 Acknowledge your contribution.
 Apologize accurately.

Day 14
(Ephesians 4:13)
Maturity

Do you have a good attitude in the midst of a bad day?

The true test of maturity is your response to difficult situations. American businessman Samuel Ullman said, *"Maturity is the ability to think, speak, and act your feelings within the bounds of dignity. The measure of your maturity is how spiritual you become during the midst of your frustrations."*

You will encounter people who cannot approach a disagreement without insulting or cursing another.

Can you disagree with someone without calling names and accusing someone?

How do you respond to the offensive acts of others?

Stresses reveal our true character.

Can you approach a disagreement with dignity?

You can influence the outcome of the conversation. Take a deep breath. Don't react. Respond maturely.

<u>Remember</u>:
In a conflict

☕ Pause.
☕ Gain perspective.
☕ Respond.

Day 15
(Psalm 139:14)
Your Difference

What makes you unique?
What is your difference?

Every life has an uncommon message.
Discover the unique message of your life.
Common is comfortable. Achievements occur
from uncommon plans and goals.

What distinguishes an uncommon achiever
from others?

An uncommon achiever seeks out those who
are successful and asks questions.
Find an expert in your desired field and
investigate his success. Take time to learn
about the success of others. Always seek. Be
a lifelong learner.

Uncommon achievers conduct themselves wisely in the presence of greatness.

Learn protocol. Behave appropriately. Dress for the occasion. Find out what behavior is expected. Do your homework. Discover your difference.

Become an uncommon achiever!

<u>Remember:</u>

☕ What is your difference?

☕ Find your uncommon message.

☕ Study to become an uncommon achiever.

Day 16
(1 Thessalonians 5:18)
Gratitude

A grateful heart is a happy heart.

Be grateful. Gratitude is a practice that can transform your day. Begin your morning with thanksgiving. Celebrate the little bright spots throughout your day.

Albert Einstein said, *"There are only two ways to live your life. One is as though nothing is a miracle. The other is as though everything is a miracle."*

It is only through gratitude that life becomes rich. Ingratitude is an impoverished mindset. At times, we must shift our focus from what we do not possess to what we do have.

Cultivate the gratitude habit.

Change your perspective. Each day is a gift. Receive it with joy.

<u>Remember:</u>

☕ Celebrate the bright spots throughout your day.

☕ Be thankful for what you have.

☕ Shift your perspective.

Day 17
(Romans 12:2)
Self-Talk

Talk to yourself.

To maintain motivation, you must exercise positive self-talk. The greatest battle you will face in regards to motivation is the battle of your mind.

Your mind is a powerful force to motivate you or deflate you. You must have the proper focus. If your mind is not future-focused, you will play and replay past failures and regrets. Destructive self-talk will cripple you. What you think, you become.

Turn off the negative internal dialog that says you are a failure, no one loves you, and you are inadequate.

Begin to confess what God says about you. You are the head and not the tail, above only and not beneath. You are more than a conqueror.

Replace negative self-talk with consistent positive thoughts. Ann Bradford said, *"Tell the negative committee that meets inside your head to sit down and shut up."*

You become what you think. Your mindset is everything. You cannot live a victorious life with defeated thinking. Your thoughts are the greatest motivation in your life.

If you do not govern your thoughts, your thoughts will govern you.

<u>Remember</u>:
Eliminate

 **Self-criticism**
Negativity
Regret

Day 18
(Proverbs 1:5)
Lifelong learner

Learn something new today.

Ben Franklin said, *"An investment in knowledge pays the best interest."*

Become a lifelong learner. Stupidity is costly. Strive to learn.

"The capacity to learn is a gift; the ability to learn is a skill; the willingness to learn is a choice." —Brian Herbert

A learning curve is essential to growth. There is always something you do not know. Find that person who knows what you don't and begin asking questions. Find an expert in your desired field and interview him. Give her a call and request some time to talk.

When you learn, you grow. No experience is wasted, if it is a learning experience. Even a failure can teach you valuable lessons.

Never stop learning.

Remember:

☕ Be curious.

☕ Ask questions.

☕ Seek to learn.

Day 19
(Philippians 4:6)
Worry

Stop worrying.

The Bible tells us to be *"anxious for nothing."* Jesus instructed us to not worry, because we cannot add one single hour to our life by worrying. Tomorrow will take care of itself.

Fretting causes harm. Anxiety, fear, and worry affect your mind and body. Fear can weaken your immune system, cause cardiovascular damage, create gastrointestinal damage, decrease fertility, diminish memory, and cause fatigue and depression.

It is important to recognize and isolate anxious thoughts, which cause cognitive distortions.

We often imagine situations to be worse than they actually are. Most often, our worries surround what could happen.

Fear encompasses the idea of danger. Ask yourself, *"Am I in real danger?"*
Imagine a positive, successful outcome.
Step away from any anxiety triggers, such as social media, news broadcasts, and horror films.

Isolate anxious thoughts.

Remember:

 Recognize anxious thoughts.
Avoid anxiety triggers.
Focus on a positive outcome.

Day 20

(Proverbs 10:20)

Uncommon Speech

Have uncommon speech.

"You will never reach the palace talking like a peasant." —Dr. Mike Murdock

Is your speech uncommon? Is your speech profane like the rest of the world? Is your speech mediocre?

An uncommon person's words have value, like choice silver. Uncommon people guard their words. Your words give life and longevity to everything spoken. Your words can build bridges or barricades. Your speech can open or close doors. Words can bring life or death. Words create conversations and transform situations.

Uncommon people realize that their words are framing their world. Words frame your future.

We often can determine where a person is from by his accent. Even greater, you can tell where a person is going by his speech.

You will have what you say.

Remember:

☕ Your words are framing your future.

☕ Words bring life or death.

☕ Words build bridges or barricades.

Day 21
(Proverbs 13:4)
Pursuit

Pursue means to follow in order to catch, attack, stalk, hound, trace, or shadow.

Pursue implies continuing a course of action with a view to its completion.

An uncommon person knows that you will never possess what you are unwilling to pursue. When you desire something that you have never had, you must do something you have never done.
There is a price to possession.

You must stalk, hound, and shadow what you desire with a focus on completion. Diligence will produce success and overcome difficulties.

Samuel Johnson said, *"Few things are impossible to diligence and skill."*

The Bible says, *"The diligent hand will rule."*
What do you want in life?
What do you desire?
Write out an action plan.
And don't give up.

Remember:

☕ You must pursue in order to possess.

☕ There is a price to possessing your dreams.

☕ Focus on completion.

Day 22
(Matthew 5:37)
Excuses

Stop making excuses!

You have a choice. You can progress, or you can make excuses. Making excuses is a habit you must stop today. It is not about having time, but about setting priorities and making time.

"He that is good for making excuses is seldom good for anything else."
—Benjamin Franklin

So, why do we make excuses?
Life coach Monica Castenetto* identifies 5 reasons why we make excuses:

1) We often aim high and make resolutions, but routine sets in.

It is easier to remain with the old, the familiar. Set the bar high and establish a new normal.

2) **Once we decide we need a change, we often allow doubt to shake our resolve.** We flounder on the decision, and excuses rescue us temporarily from the doubt.

3) **We become afraid—afraid of risk and change.** We are afraid to fail, to be judged, to be rejected, or make a mistake. No one enjoys feeling afraid, so we make excuses.

4) **We are not ready.**

5) **We are just not motivated enough.**

Excuses are rationalizations we make to ourselves to defend a behavior, procrastinate an action, or neglect our responsibility. Excuses prevent you from living your best at your full potential.

Be accountable.
Be responsible.

Stop making excuses!

Remember:
Why do we make excuses?

☕ **To defend a behavior.**

☕ **Procrastinate an action.**

☕ **Neglect responsibility.**

For more information on Monica Castenetto visit:
https://livealifeyoulove.co.uk

Notes:

Day 23
(Matthew 5:16)
Influence

In any given place, there is a person of influence.

Is the person of influence within a corporation or organization always the person with a title? No. The person with influence is not always the boss.

Take a look around your workplace.
Who is influential? Is it you?
Could it be you? **YES!**

Important endeavors cannot be accomplished without the ability to capture the hearts, minds, and energy of those around you. Effective leaders do not manipulate or dictate. They inspire, persuade, and encourage.

Great leaders influence others.

*"True leadership comes only from influence.
A title cannot buy influence."*
— John C. Maxwell

Effective leadership involves great character, relationships, and knowledge. Character begins with the inner person. Relationships increase loyalty and influence. Cultivate meaningful relationships within your organization or work. Knowledge is important.
Do your homework before you take the lead.

Learn first, then lead.

<u>Remember:</u>
Factors of Influence

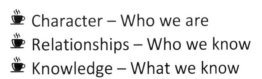 Character – Who we are
☕ Relationships – Who we know
☕ Knowledge – What we know

Day 24
(1 Corinthians 13:11)
Personal Growth

You will experience change in your life.

Change is inevitable, but will YOU change?
Will you grow?
"Every moment of one's existence, one is growing into more or retreating into less."
— Norman Mailer

Life is growth.
Will you choose to grow through the challenges?
Through the heartache and the conflict?

True progression is being superior to your former self. Growth is a determining factor between those who succeed and those who don't. Personal growth is not automatic or haphazard.

Identify where you need to grow. Gather useful information on the topic. Conduct a Bible study on the subject and meditate on scripture.

Schedule time every day for personal growth.

Remember:
For personal growth:

☕ Identify where you need to grow.

☕ Make personal growth a daily priority.

☕ Make a plan that is specific and scheduled.

Day 25
(Jeremiah 29:11)
Purpose

Before you do anything, you need to discover your purpose.

You cannot reach a sense of fulfillment in life without knowing your purpose.

Dr. Paul Crites in his book, *Discovering the Power of Purpose*, outlines 4 questions to reveal your purpose. Ask yourself:

1) **What do you love?**
   This reveals a gift that God has placed in your life. What you love encompasses your difference, your uniqueness. Begin focusing on what you love!

2) **What do you hate?**

This reveals what you are called to correct. The problem that infuriates you is the problem you are called to solve.

3) What makes you cry?
This reveals what you are called to heal. What saddens you is a sign of your purpose.

4) What annoys or irritates you?
What annoys you reveals what kind of people will be drawn to you. Your purpose is a specific answer to specific problems.

<u>Remember</u>:
Write it down!

☕ What do you love?
☕ What do you hate?
☕ What makes you cry?
☕ What annoys you?

For more information on Purpose: paulcrites.com

Day 26
(Jeremiah 1:9)
Authentic Voice

The world needs to hear your story.

You must realize that you aren't called to everyone; you are called to someone. We cannot possibly know and master everything. Pick a lane.

Scattered focus hinders progress. When you are moving in too many directions, you become ineffective, fatigued, and frustrated.

What is your unique purpose and assignment? Discover your difference.

Knowing your specific voice and purpose places you on the fast track for success. Within you is a power to find and express your own unique message.

If you do not define your story, the world will define your story for you.
Discover your unique purpose...your difference...your voice...your story.

Remember:

☕ You aren't called to everyone.

☕ Pick a lane.

☕ Discover your difference. Find your voice.

Day 27
(Psalm 133:1)
Teamwork

Relationships are key to success.

Specifically, building a team is key to achieving goals.

"Talent wins games, but teamwork and intelligence wins championships."
                    –Michael Jordan

An effective team can take you to the next level of accomplishment. It works in all aspects of life from an executive team to family chores at home. It is so much easier to finish a task with others, if you get them on your team.

Be enthusiastic.
Be convincing.

Make them want to join you. Make the job fun! Who wants to be on a team that is replete with drudgery and negativity?

If you are unable to establish a team or keep others on your team, ask why. Together you can achieve more and go farther. Teamwork divides the load, but multiplies the success.

We cannot win unless we play together.

<u>Remember</u>:
To create a team

☕ Motivate-provide incentives.

☕ Inspire-be positive.

☕ Encourage-reward accomplishment.

Day 28
(Proverbs 11:12)
Fault finding

Stop focusing on the flaws of others and catch them doing something right.

Relationships are key to success. You need right relationships! Often, we default to automatically recognizing and emphasizing the shortcomings of people, especially those close to us. We become too familiar with individuals and fail to acknowledge, praise, or be grateful for the good qualities that the person adds to the workplace or home.

How can we change a critical default?

Praise others publicly and privately. Recognize completed tasks and good attitudes.

Be swift to reward people who help you achieve a goal.

What you look at the longest, becomes the strongest. Consequently, if you are focusing on the faults of others, the flaws will obscure the positive qualities.

We have a tendency to believe that everyone's faults are so much greater than our own. Stop spending so much time focusing on others' flaws and work on your own.

Do you have a critical focus?

<u>Remember:</u>

- ☕ Change your focus.
- ☕ Recognize the good qualities of others.
- ☕ Praise others publicly and privately.

Day 29
(Proverbs 12:24)
Daily routine

The secret of your future is hidden in your daily routine.

In fact, I can predict your future by examining your daily habits. Your destiny is being shaped day by day. What you are doing daily is shaping what you are becoming permanently.

Habits are either moving you toward your goal or away from your goal. Men rarely choose their future, but men daily choose their routines.

Sit down and map out your day/week/ month. Purchase a day planner. Be selective with whom you grant time. Create and keep a schedule.

What do you want to accomplish today?
☑ Write it down.

What tasks need to be completed in order to achieve that goal?
☑ Prioritize those tasks.

☠ Do not allow people to steal valuable time from your day. Put your phone on voice mail to avoid getting caught in lengthy conversations.

If you do talk to someone, set a time limit for the conversation and stick to it. Send an email or text to save time.

Your daily routine is shaping your future.

<u>Remember:</u>

☕ Write out a daily schedule.
☕ Don't allow others to waste your time.
☕ Prioritize your tasks.

Day 30
(Proverbs 15:31-33)
Criticism

Criticism from others is a chance to learn.

How you handle criticism is an indication of your maturity and emotional intelligence.

Criticism is everywhere, but we don't listen to all of it. Consider the source. Some criticism you can throw out. Evaluate criticism from respected sources, which gives you a window into how others think.

Do not allow your emotions to close your mind and cause you to become immediately defensive. When you receive negative feedback, ask how this can make you better. Ask the person why he feels this way. And listen. Don't miss the opportunity to grow.

Be proactive, not reactive.

Put feelings aside and consider how you can learn from this new perspective.

<u>Remember</u>:
Criticism is

☕ An opportunity to grow.

☕ A chance to learn.

☕ A window into how others think.

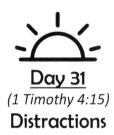

Day 31
(1 Timothy 4:15)

Distractions

Distract means to draw or drag apart.

When you are distracted, you are drawn apart. Your mind becomes diverted, and your focus is divided.

Focus determines your success and decides your destiny. Your focus is everything, but distractions are everywhere. You cannot accomplish great things, if you are distracted by small things.

Starve your distractions.

What distracts us?
Wrong relationships, cell phones, social media—anything that wastes your energy.

Distractions destroy action.

Fundamental to your success is choosing what NOT to do.

"When a person cannot find a deep sense of meaning, he distracts himself with pleasure."
— Viktor Frankl

Many times in my life, I have been unfocused and distracted. I had intentions, but no actions. I had wishes, but no goals. My free time was unfocused, and my daily routine consisted of trying to survive the day.

Put away your distractions and focus your life.

Your focus is everything!

Remember to avoid distractions:

- Turn off your phone.
- Prioritize your work. Do the most important first.
- Train your mind by meditating on God's Word.

Beyond Publishing & Promotions – USA

Daily Dose Devotional Series
Copyright © 2019
ISBN: 978-1-64621-005-3

 April Williams is an author, speaker, librarian, manager, wife, and mother of five sons. She hosts a morning broadcast on Facebook called *Daily Dose LIVE*.

She is also the Worship Leader at Beyond Church in Lancaster, South Carolina. When April is not working, she loves a cup of green tea while watching *Pride & Prejudice*. And chocolate... chocolate is always appropriate.

For more information, visit
wisdomforbeyond.com

For booking information contact:
mydailydoselive@gmail.com